# DIGGING DEEP

---

## FINDING TREASURE IN DARK PLACES

## KRISTIN GAULT

Print ISBN: 978-1-952385-50-6

eBook ISBN: 978-1-952385-51-3

Published by Above The Sun, LLC

Cover Designed by Get Covers

Scripture quotations marked (NIV) are taken from the Holy Bible, New
International Version®, NIV®. Copyright © 1973, 1978, 1984, 2011 by Biblica, Inc.™
Used by permission of Zondervan. All rights reserved worldwide.
www.zondervan.com The "NIV" and "New International Version" are
trademarks registered in the United States Patent and Trademark Office by
Biblica, Inc.™

Scripture quotations marked (TPT) are from The Passion Translation®.
Copyright © 2017, 2018 by Passion & Fire Ministries, Inc. Used by permission.
All rights reserved. ThePassionTranslation.com.

Scripture quotations marked (ESV) are from The ESV® Bible (The Holy Bible,
English Standard Version®), copyright © 2001 by Crossway, a publishing
ministry of Good News Publishers. Used by permission. All rights reserved.

Scripture quotations marked (AMP) are taken from the AMPLIFIED® BIBLE,
Copyright© 1954, 1958, 1962, 1964, 1965, 1987 by the Lockman Foundation Used by
Permission. (www.Lockman.org)

The Christian Standard Bible. Copyright © 2017 by Holman Bible Publishers.
Used by permission. Christian Standard Bible®, and CSB® are federally
registered trademarks of Holman Bible Publishers, all rights reserved.

This book has been produced in association with Above The Sun, LLC, which
has a mission to help authors release heaven through their authentic stories.
For author coaching or publishing advice, learn more at https://
abovethesun.org.

# CONTENTS

*This book is dedicated to all those who are struggling, to those who are in a tough spot. Keep moving forward, step by step. Don't give up. We will walk this road together. You are not alone.*

*"How enriched are they who find their strength in the Lord; within their hearts are the highways of holiness! Even when their paths wind through the dark valley of tears, they dig deep to find a pleasant pool where others find only pain. He gives to them a brook of blessing filled from the rain of an outpouring. They grow stronger and stronger with every step forward, and the God of all gods will appear before them in Zion." (Psalm 84:5–7, TPT)*

*"Lord, take me deeper than my feet could ever travel ..."*

# INTRODUCTION

2024 was a very difficult year for our family. It started with an ice storm that significantly damaged our house, then to living apart for the next five months while our house was going through major repairs. We moved back in at the beginning of summer. The summer entailed working a new schedule, publishing my first book, and then walking the 200-mile trek known as "El Camino" only to return and go to my first work training for the new school year the next day.

I got to a point where my body finally ungracefully let me know "enough is enough."

I had just returned from my journey walking El Camino from Porto, Portugal, to Santiago de Compostela in Spain. This trip took me by surprise as what was supposed to be pure adventure ended up being more difficult than I could have imagined. As I reached my limits physically and mentally, I was forced to dig deeper than ever before to keep going to make it to the finish line. (More about this in Chapter 2.)

In reflecting back on these intense situations, this concept of *digging deep* really struck a chord in me. It involves using all our resources to accomplish something. This encompasses deep soul searching through introspection. It's that exploration of those inner thoughts, feelings and motivations for why we do what we do. We find resilience and strength as we look inside ourselves to overcome obstacles and realize our potential in the process. Most importantly, digging deeper into our relationship with Jesus Christ and who we are in him, into his promises toward us, provides us with the *why* we are here on this earth. It gives meaning to all we go through in this life.

The front cover of this book may not show a literal picture of me digging a hole. I have just hit mile seventy of El Camino and am digging deep within myself to just keep moving forward. At this point I am experiencing intense pain in my feet and legs. Simultaneously, my body's reaction to the heat and humidity have caused rashes up and down my arms and legs that have produced tiny blisters. I cannot see what is ahead of me beyond ten feet. But despite all this pain, something deep inside pushes my body forward. And when I travail on, I discover a deep treasure. A treasure I have come to realize could only be discovered by going through difficulty and adversity.

This is how life works.

I discovered this treasure by digging. Through this process, the treasure comes to the surface often in a revelation or insight. Other times it just shows up through the words of others or just through the process of overcoming. This treasure is always a gift, often materializing in surprising ways.

Now, after being back, with the previous challenges behind me, I find myself in a similar spot where I am having to dig deep again. I can't see what is ahead of me very far. All I know is I need to keep going. Step by step. At times it feels like it's only baby steps. But I keep going forward, trusting. As I go forward, I walk in the shadow of the Almighty. I am protected.

I had the desire to start writing again. My first thought was to write about my adventure on El Camino, but when I brainstormed with my publisher, interestingly enough, what came out of that session was not just one, but two more books. One would have the specifics of that journey, but, as we talked, this larger concept of digging deep emerged. We decided that I would also write a book about finding treasure to go along with the agate theme from my first book, *Gifts of Sight*.

Something about this struck deep within me.

The following week reflecting on this, I realized that right now I do find myself digging deep again, just to keep going. Digging deep to find the joy in the small mundane moments of life. Trying to keep in mind the reasons I do anything, the purpose behind what I do. I don't know what God has ahead for me, but all I know is I am clinging to Him now just to keep my head up day by day.

If that is where you find yourself, join me in this journey. You are not alone. Life always changes and sometimes these changes creep up and hit hard. As I share about where I had to dig deep to find treasure, my hope is you will be able to dig with me and find your own treasure.

*"Therefore we do not give up. Even though our outer person is being destroyed, our inner person is being renewed day by day. For our momentary light affliction is producing for us an absolutely incomparable eternal weight of glory. So we do not focus on what is seen, but on what is unseen. For what is seen is temporary, but what is unseen is eternal."*
2 Corinthians 4:16–18 (CSB)

*"My goal is that they may be encouraged in heart and united in love, so that they may have the full riches of complete understanding, in order that they may know the mystery of God, namely, Christ, in whom are hidden all the treasures of wisdom and knowledge."*
Colossians 2:2–3 (NIV)

# 1

# THE ICE STORM

**January 13, 2024**

I woke up early to have some quiet time with God before the rest of the family got up.

The weather forecast told us to prepare for an ice storm. Everyone was hunkered down with food and water, and propane in case the power went out. The electrical company had come out the day before to reinforce the pole on our driveway responsible for carrying electricity to our house as well as our neighbors' houses. Preparations were being made everywhere, and we were ready. It was beautiful outside and very quiet. Like the calm before the storm. It made it feel very cozy inside.

I had been reading Haley Braun's book *Surrendered to the Holy Spirit*, along with a devotional from Lectio 365 that seemed to match up with the book. It was about being in the wilderness and being shaken up so that what remains is that which cannot be shaken. One of the focuses was on shaking up fear until fear falls away, replaced by complete trust in God.

Overcoming fear is a theme in my book *Gifts of Sight*, and I was finding meaning in scriptures given that morning.

My aim for this time was to start writing my epilogue for my book *Gifts of Sight*, tasked with the goal of bringing everything together. Before starting, I reminded myself of Psalm 139:3–5 (tpt): "You are so intimately aware of me, Lord. You read my heart like an open book and you know all the words I'm about to speak [write] before I even start a sentence! You know every step I will take before my journey even begins. You've gone into my future to prepare the way, and in kindness you follow behind me to spare me from the harm of my past. You have laid your hand on me!" It gave me confidence knowing he was writing with me. God abiding in me, me abiding in God. We were one.

After a couple hours, my husband, Jon, and son Peter both woke up and came out. My other son, Reilly, was at a conference in Southern California and my daughter, Paige, was staying in her dorm at college since it was too dangerous to drive home on the roads.

It was just us three.

We ventured outside wearing crampons on our boots because the ice was already thick. I took pictures as we oohed and aahed over the beauty of ice-encrusted leaves on plants. We could hear branches start to crack so we headed back inside.

Around midmorning our power went out.

Jon and I got our boots back on and used ski poles to make our way down the hill, where we witnessed a large tree down over our driveway that had knocked out the newly fortified power pole. Fortunately for us, it was early in the storm and the electric company was able to come and move the tree off our driveway so we could still get out.

We met our elderly neighbor in the driveway and got him set up with a way to stay warm in his kitchen before heading back to our house.

Jon stayed outside to hook up the propane tank to get the generator going. Peter was inside using the bathroom.

About five minutes later, Peter came out and we heard Jon scream, "Nooooooo!"

Time froze.

I had no idea where Jon was, if he was in danger of getting hit. I didn't know what was going on, but knew it was not good.

Then the boom came, and the house shook. Glass shattered in the bathroom where Peter had just been. We were hit. Then it was quiet.

I didn't know if Jon had gotten hit by the tree. I rushed to the kitchen window screaming Jon's name at the same time he began screaming mine.

Mercifully, all three of us were fine. We could breathe again.

Jon came in the back door, and we walked through the house together to survey the damage. It was eerie. Great spears of branches broke through the ceiling in several places. The bathroom window was shattered, and a ten-foot limb had broken right through to the toilet, shattering the shelf above it and taking out the light, missing the plumbing by mere centimeters.

Right where Peter had been.

Spears were coming through the shower, the hallway, the kitchen, the front porch. It felt like we had been invaded.

Jon immediately went out to get a ladder to put a tarp on the roof to cover all the holes. I was in strong disagreement as trees were now coming down all around us with branches breaking off. It was getting darker as the winter days were short.

Despite the disagreement, Jon went up on the roof while my job was to keep an eye out for falling trees. Two more trees fell on the dining room side of the house while he was on the roof on the other side. Thoughts of becoming a widow terrorized me, and all I could do was just cry out for God's protection.

We prepared ourselves to hunker down for the night, trying to patch up the holes as best we could to conserve what heat we had, although our house was already in the low thirties. Luckily, we still had cell service and were able to let friends and family know what was happening. Meanwhile more trees had fallen in our driveway, trapping us from getting out or allowing any help to come to us.

That night was the longest night I have ever experienced. The sounds of trees breaking all around us went on throughout the extended hours. Several more trees hit throughout the night. One time was by our bedroom wall, pulling the main power source away from the house.

Jon had to go out every three hours to refill the generator with propane since it was a small tank, only enough to keep our phones charged and run our small fireplace as a heater. Every time he ventured outside, it was with the risk of getting hit by a 2,000-pound tree.

Around 3:00 a.m., I remember singing songs to Jesus in a shaky voice, just to keep the terror at bay.

Morning came, and we ventured out to survey the damage. We could barely get out the back door because trees had fallen on that side. The front door had a spear right above it, and the porch had another large spear that went through, breaking the bench that was sitting there—the branch more than ten feet long.

Ice lay inches thick on the driveway. The part of the driveway that was less steep was inaccessible due to the trees that had fallen. Our only way of escape was down the steep hill.

Jon got out the rest of our supply of salt, and with our shovels we slowly worked our way down to the bottom of our hill to where our gate was. After hours spent breaking up the ice, we made it, only to find the rest of the driveway completely blocked with additional trees.

Our neighbor had a massive fir tree that fell right through his living room, leaving his home open to the elements. Looking at our house from his property, we could see our garage had been hit, and spears had gotten through to the inside there as well.

We called friends for help only to find out the highway was closed on both sides because fallen trees blocked the road.

The realization we were stuck and help was unavailable brought on more waves of fear. A second long night loomed ahead of us while tree branches continued to fall. Meanwhile, we heard another ice storm was on its way.

We decided my job was to call around to find a tree company who could come help. I made multiple calls only to find out everyone was either already booked or not available. Then a good friend reached out to a local tree company where she knew the owners. I went through the motions of calling again, and this time a friendly voice answered the phone. I burst into tears asking for help.

Because of our intensely dangerous situation, this tree company bumped us up to the front of the line, as soon as the highway was open. When they came, they advised us to get out before the next ice storm hit since there were at least ten more eighty-foot-plus Douglas firs that posed a threat to our home.

With nowhere for our dogs to go, Jon was determined to stay. I did not want him to stay alone, so, when the road was cleared, friends came and picked Peter up at the bottom of the driveway while bringing us more supplies to make it through a second night. Our neighbor's family also came and picked the elderly man up, not realizing it would be eleven months before he would be back living in his home.

That second night passed with no trees falling on the house, thankfully. But the weather predicted the second ice storm was coming the following night. We spent the day trying to clear paths. Jon moved our bus out of the path of a threatening tree. The tree company called to check up on us and to encourage Jon to leave the house and stay somewhere safe.

As evening approached, Jon was still convinced he was going to stay with the dogs. I was put in the position, again, of having to choose between staying with my husband or going someplace safe. As the temperature dropped and the cracking of trees and branches commenced yet again, I struggled with deep fear. I felt I had to choose between my husband and my kids. A horrible position to be in. If I stayed with Jon, there would be a possibility that our kids would lose us both. For that reason, I put my things together and slid down our driveway so friends could come pick me up, and left to be with Peter.

Meanwhile, at our friends' house, the real cracking began. It sounded like a war was going on around us. The branches blasted like guns going off as they broke. Echoes of deep thuds, cracks, and crashes reverberated as trees fell against houses, cars, and fences, breaking through.

I stayed in contact with Jon. During the late evening, other friends nearby who'd heard about our situation called and offered their garage as a place for our dogs to stay, which allowed Jon the ability to leave. While on the phone letting him know our friend's invitation, he witnessed three more eighty-foot trees fall on our neighbor's property.

He decided to get out.

The next morning, we discovered, miraculously, the ten trees that were threatening our house and leaning over more and more with the weight of the ice, never touched our home. It was the power of prayer. We had many people praying protection over our home, and God answered. Our huge maple tree lost most of its branches, covering the rest of our driveway and narrowly missing the bus.

God is good.

The next six months we spent repairing the home to make it livable again. The company working with us predicted only seven trusses had broken from looking at the outside of the house. Seventeen were later found broken. The roof had to come off, the framing redone, some walls rebuilt, a new window installed, holes filled, and flooring replaced. Jon stayed on the property in our trailer with the dogs while Peter and I stayed with friends in their rental space.

We were able to move back in the beginning of summer as school got out. There were still many projects to finish including the flooring, but it was livable and we needed to be together as a family.

Through it all, life never slowed down. Work still had its demands. People had their expectations. Meanwhile the feelings and emotions of what happened were pushed down, ignored.

Life goes on. Or does it?

**Digging Deep**

Finally taking time to process this experience, I find myself asking God what is it he wants me to take from this? Where are the treasures to be found from this experience?

First and foremost, we were unharmed. Our pets were unharmed. Treasure.

Friendship and sacrifice. People who prayed for us, friends who gave us a place to stay, a place for our pets. The insurance company and the restoration company, along with the tree company coming to our aid quickly. Treasure.

Treasure in looking back and recognizing all the ways God provided for our needs. We were never alone. There was blessing poured out on us despite the devastation.

Have you experienced an ice storm of sorts in your life?

Have you been displaced due to unforeseen circumstances? This could be through a natural disaster, war, death, relationship difficulties, etc. Something beyond your control.

If so, take heart and realize that you are not alone.

I encourage you to look for the treasures in your dark place. Look for the people who have stuck around in the middle of your pain. And if there is no one, then know that God has never left you.

## 2

# EL CAMINO

El Camino consists of a series of ancient routes that lead to Santiago de Compostela in Spain. For thousands of years, people have walked these routes for religious reasons as an act of devotion or obedience within the Catholic faith. But there have been others who have walked for other personal reasons, whether these be adventure, a unique way to explore a new country, a need to process grief, a way to transition a big life change, etc.

My friend Heather and I had been planning this trip since the summer of 2023, before the ice storm. Our reasons for completing this walk were primarily for adventure and to explore this part of the world. The direction we chose to walk was the Portuguese route starting in Porto, Portugal.

Our trip was planned for the latter half of August 2024. The timing was influenced by incredibly discounted airline tickets we couldn't turn down as well as my work schedule. We had bought these tickets in December 2023. Our first training walk for this adventure was on a local path January 1, 2024—twelve days before the ice storm.

Throughout the months following the storm, I found the preparation for this trip grounded me and helped me hold onto something the storm hadn't taken away. It gave me hope that life would return to normal.

Much preparation went into walking El Camino. We had, roughly, twelve days to walk two hundred miles to get to our destination. A large amount of time went into research on backpacks, clothing, sleeping gear, sleeping arrangements, local culture, weather, etc. Everything we brought had to be carried on our backs for these two hundred miles and carefully thought through beforehand. Our goal was to keep our backpack weight to around ten pounds. It was essential we had the right footgear. We made multiple trips to REI to try out different shoes, backpacks, even walking poles.

Our training walks slowly increased in length and time, often taking up four to five hours. Throughout this time, excitement grew. The house repairs and living separately as a family took a toll, but this trip was something positive to focus on. Portugal and Spain were both countries I had always longed to visit, and I could hardly wait to get on the plane.

Interestingly enough, what started out as an adventure turned out to be a true pilgrimage as this walk ended up being one of the hardest physical challenges I have gone through in my life. It pushed me to reach my limits physically and mentally. The reality of El Camino and what transpired during those twelve days caught us both entirely by surprise since it was completely unexpected. What happened was not due to a lack of being prepared. But life can hit like that and, despite all foresight and precautions taken, you can be blindsided.

By the second day, I dealt with the agony of muscle spasms all up and down my right leg and hives and heat blisters throughout my body. This was coupled with swollen ankles and feet from retaining water, which resulted in blisters upon blisters on both feet. Every morning commenced with pain shooting everywhere beginning from the first step and the knowledge that I had to complete nineteen to twenty-some miles that day.

Step by step, dealing with immense pain was the only way forward.

Ironically, the pain, in a way, grounded me. It forced me to be completely present. And through this pain, I discovered deep joy. Joy not in the happy bubbly sense, but in feeling so alive. Supernatural joy in taking in the beauty of my surroundings.

The front cover of this book shows me walking along a cobblestoned Roman path thousands of years old, walls on both sides of me. The heat and humidity were relentless. However, I had a special umbrella that not only gave me shade, it also created a cool environment beneath it, supposedly cooling the outside temperature by fifteen degrees. At times, I could not see what was ahead of me beyond the next ten feet. All I knew was that I needed to keep on going. Step by step. I had to dig deeper than ever before to keep going to make it to the finish line.

In the midst of digging deep, finding strength from the depths of my being, and forcing myself to continuously move forward, there was this deep joy and anticipation in discovering treasures around every bend. The path ahead often had a turn, and one never knew what would be found beyond the turn. It could be an open vista of a town with red-tiled roofs overlooking the blue ocean, a Roman bridge built centuries ago, the narrow cobblestoned street of a town, an old Gothic-looking church, or the entrance into another enchanting eucalyptus forest.

Riches unimaginable would turn up in the form of the landscape or in the form of other people I would run into. Unexpected kindnesses, the sacrificial giving of my friend on my behalf, or finding myself in the midst of rich cultural experiences. All gems.

At the time I did not recognize the personal significance of all the eucalyptus forests we encountered along the way. When I got back home, I happened upon a letter a friend had written to me a year earlier. It was not a coincidence that eucalyptus leaves were printed in the background. In her note she explained that eucalyptus stood for strength, protection, and abundance.

In the midst of my walk and dealing with the pain, I wasn't aware of what God was providing me with minute by minute. It was through looking back that I was overwhelmed by this reality. By the grace of God, I was able to finish this walk because I was provided with an abundance of strength and protection again and again and again.

Sometimes it takes looking back to discover the treasure.

## Digging Deep

There was a pervasive sense throughout my journey that I was being prepared for something ahead where I would also have to dig deep. Not in the physical sense, but in an emotional and spiritual sense. I believe that going through the experience of El Camino and overcoming all the obstacles that were put before me and my friend was something God was gifting me with to prepare me for what was to come.

The physical, emotional, mental, and spiritual aspects of ourselves are all tied together, each impacting the other. This is why Jesus tells us to love God with all our heart, mind, soul, and strength. My physical experience had a direct impact on teaching me how resilient I was in all areas of my life.

Have you gone through a physical experience where there was struggle involved to make it through? Maybe through the training for and completion of an event. Maybe it was an illness or chronic pain. What have you learned about yourself through this struggle, and how has it impacted other areas of your life? Has it made you stronger? Has it made you more dependent on God? Has it increased your awareness of God's presence in your life?

Have there been times in your life where in the moment you may not have been in a place to recognize the treasures being given to you? I encourage you to take some time to look back and see if you can recognize treasures that before were hidden.

Look to see if you can recognize the treasures of God's faithfulness seeing you through, helping you overcome.

# 3

# PARALYSIS

Paralyzed. Frozen.

Feeling like a deer caught in the headlights. This is how my school year started the fall of 2024.

I had gotten back from Portugal the night before my first full day of training. I arrived home on a Tuesday evening and reported to work at 8:00 a.m. Wednesday morning. I have had to dig deep even since then, just on a different level.

Dealing with sleep deprivation and working through physical pain and the aftermath of what my body had gone through, I started the school year. With no break or period of recuperation, it was full steam ahead into working with students.

I felt like I couldn't think of what to do with my students. My mind was completely blank. Feelings of incompetence and loss of confidence surrounded me. I found myself wondering what I was doing in my position of working with these kids. Erroneous perceptions swirled inside me, accusing me of being an imposter.

And it didn't stop there.

These feelings extended to my home. It was like I forgot how to clean and pick up the house. I was completely overwhelmed by everyday tasks, not knowing where to start. The thought of going grocery shopping was terrifying. It's like I had no idea what to get or what to cook.

Because of the devastation from the ice storm, piles of flooring, a kitchen sink, lighting fixtures, etc., took up residence in our hallway, living room, and dining room. Our bedroom and bathroom still needed the flooring done. Kitchen counters needed to be torn out and replaced, cupboards and trim painted. The lighting fixtures in the kids' bathroom were still broken from the tree limbs piercing through the roof from the storm months ago.

It all contributed to my feeling paralyzed, not knowing where to start or what to do.

When I shared what I was going through with some close friends, one sent me information on the reasons for why one is feeling this way. She shared in her research that paralysis is one of the ways our body responds to stress. One's autonomic nervous system—also known as the fight, flight, or freeze response—gets activated. The freeze response can feel like paralysis, affecting one's physical, emotional, and cognitive self.

## The Beginning of the School Year

As I write these words, I have just finished another work week where I sludged through the motions. There have been big changes at work, including major budget cuts where our staffing was cut short. Our job that had been accomplished through four teachers is now down to three. Caseloads have risen.

Most of my classrooms have new teachers and new staff, many inexperienced in working with students with complex needs. Some of my students have moved into classrooms that have nothing. Literally. The previous teachers had taken everything with them. The shelves are bare, with no books, no activity materials of any sort. Aides are new, and besides meeting basic needs, they do not know what to do with the students.

This is where I find myself at the present. Facing these challenges while feeling I have nothing to give. I am told that classrooms are looking forward to having the "vision specialist" come visit, thinking I will provide answers and solutions to problematic behaviors of my students, assuming they have to do with lack of vision.

I wake up in the mornings and look at my schedule for the day. I see the schools and homes I will be walking into. What if nothing comes to mind? What if the vision specialist part of who I am is absent?

Instead of looking forward to the week, which has been my norm for most of my career, I find myself dreading Monday. A new feeling of panic wells up within. How am I going to get everything done that needs to be done? How am I going to meet the needs of my students?

I just found out we have several new referrals. One is more than an hour's drive away. I feel like I am drowning.

An aura starts, and a migraine rushes in. Migraines were something I had grown up with, but they had miraculously disappeared the last several years after a friend prayed over them. They are not ordinary migraines, but ones where I lose my vision, the feeling in one side of my body, and my ability to think clearly as well as the ability to communicate. It can be terrifying if I am in a place where no one really knows me. After two years of reprieve, I have had three in the last month.

## The God Who Is with Me Through It All

One morning while reading my Bible desperately searching for comfort, I was led to the familiar Psalm 23, verse 4: "Even though I walk through the darkest valley, I will fear no evil, for you are with me; your rod and your staff, they comfort me (NIV)."

God doesn't always deliver us *out* of our circumstances, but oftentimes he takes us *through* them.

"But we have this *precious* treasure [the good news about salvation] in [unworthy] earthen vessels [of human frailty], so that the grandeur *and* surpassing greatness of the power will be [shown to be] from God [His sufficiency] and not from ourselves. We are pressured in every way [hedged in], but not crushed; perplexed [unsure of finding a way out], but not driven to despair; hunted down *and* persecuted, but not deserted [to stand alone]; struck down, but never destroyed" (2 Corinthians 4:7–9, AMP).

Verse 7 jumped out at me from the Amplified Version. I am on this search for treasure, for all things good, in the midst of all that is happening in my life.

It hit me.

The treasure that really matters is already inside me. Jesus. All else pales in comparison. I can get through this because he lives in me! I can hold onto his promises that no matter what happens to me, I will not be crushed, driven to despair, deserted, or destroyed.

## Glimpses of God

"You will seek me and find me, when you seek me with all your heart. I will be found by you" (Jeremiah 29:13–14, ESV).

Last week a friend, whom I shared my struggles with, told me she felt God show her a picture of me as a blind person with a cane. The cane allowed me to go forward step by step. I was not able to see into the distance at all to know what was ahead of me, but had to trust the cane, one step at a time.

She also had this image of God playing hide-and-seek with me. Playing on purpose because he knew I would seek him and find him. Another friend present added that it was to be a hide-and-seek game as with a three-year-old, where the three-year-old hides in plain sight. God would be in plain sight all the time, "hiding" from me and waiting to be found.

The important thing to remember was that he is always present.

With this in mind, I started to go through my day keeping my eyes open for glimpses of God to keep me going. I felt I had learned this before, to find God in the small things of everyday life. But sometimes we need to relearn what we once knew—a refresher course.

At the end of the day, I would look back through my day to see where God might have been hiding. It could be as natural as the warmth of the sun to the encouraging text from a friend. Or even a friendly smile from a stranger. One day it was unexpectedly running into another teacher I had been meaning to contact. Another day it was realizing that I still had the strength to reach out and let a friend know I was thinking about them.

Seemingly small stuff, but God was in each one, hiding in plain view.

## Digging Deep

Driving to work one morning I found myself talking to God about the students I would be seeing that day. It all felt like I was walking out on a limb, taking a risk, since I didn't know if my mind would be open to getting ideas or would draw a blank again. As I was talking to God about my fear, I told him that no matter what happened, I would trust him.

The song comes on the radio randomly, "I Will Rejoice in the Lord." Something hits deep in my core. This is my song for this season. I will grab hold of it and not let go. It anchors me and holds me.

I will continue to search daily for God, but even if I don't find him, I will choose to believe and rejoice.

I will rejoice in the Lord when I don't see my "crops" producing fruit.

I will rejoice in the Lord even when I feel stagnant and am not moving, when my brain does not seem to produce thoughts or ideas, but instead appears empty.

I will rejoice in the Lord when discouragement and not seeing the end floods my soul.

I will rejoice in the Lord when I don't see the solutions to what I am facing.

I will still rejoice.

Dear reader, maybe you find yourself in a place where you feel overwhelmed. Work, relationships, physical hardships, and financial struggles all can cause stress. There are times when problems appear larger than they really are. In the midst of these times, our minds can get the best of us and lead us to dark places. It is when we are in these dark places that we have a choice to remain there, or to decide to trust God even when we may not sense him working.

Recently I reread the story of Elijah and the widow (1 Kings 17:8–14). The widow was preparing her last meal for herself and her son, expecting to die shortly after from starvation. Elijah asks her to feed him, and then tells her she will not run out of food. She did as he asked and discovered her jar of oil and container of flour never ran out. There was always enough.

Yet again, I found God hiding in plain view through this story. In this season in life, I am discovering God is providing for all my needs, even when it seems I have no reserves. He is always faithful.

I want to encourage you to trust God to provide for your needs, just as he did for the widow. She took a risk in obeying Elijah and feeding him. She had to trust what he said was true and that God would provide. And God did. Again and again until the famine was over.

*"Though the fig tree does not blossom*
*And there is no fruit on the vines,*
*Though the yield of the olive fails*
*And the fields produce no food,*
*Though the flock is cut off from the fold*
*And there are no cattle in the stalls,*
*Yet I will [choose to] rejoice in the Lord;*
*I will [choose to] shout in exultation in the [victorious] God of my*
*salvation!"*
Habakkuk 3:17–18 (AMP)

# 4

# PILES OF STUFF

It's been three months since we moved back. Summer has passed, and school has started. With both of our demanding jobs, there isn't time or space to work on the house.

Packages of flooring lie in the hallway as well as loose bits in the living room next to the fireplace. Additional piles of bathroom flooring are found in the dining room next to our new sink along with two light fixtures.

With the help of our friends, the majority of our floors have been completed. To celebrate, we bought our first robot vacuum, whom we affectionately named Jeremy. Jeremy kept getting caught trying to clean around the piles of remaining floor boards. I was always surprised at his determination to clean into every little crevice he could find and a bit impressed he never got stuck in the process.

Our bedroom and bathroom flooring still need to be done, hence the flooring in the house. It patiently lies there just waiting to be installed.

This just adds to the piles of stuff to be organized and gone through in our bedroom. Stuff that has been there for years.

The Aymara word for "stuff" is *kachi wachi*. I love this word as it provides some humor to the situation.

Because life is busy and priorities are elsewhere, one gets used to the piles. After a while they aren't even noticed. One just steps around them and goes on with the daily routine. It all becomes part of the landscape.

After coming back from Portugal, these piles started screaming for my attention. They were calling out my name for me to place them in their spot. But how? With no time and totally dependent on others to prioritize and help, I couldn't make anything happen on my own.

Walking endless hours lost in my thoughts on El Camino, I had a chance to look back at my life, my relationships. Unhealthy habits that have formed from years of practice. Is this current trial a chance at becoming new again? Could the disarray of the house actually be a gift in disguise, a chance to get a restart?

## The Business of Life

Raising kids has been one of our biggest blessings and joys. But with life happening, our priority for each other has, at times, been put on the back burner bit by bit without us realizing it.

Now with two kids in college and one finishing high school, my husband and I are looking at becoming empty nesters.

The thought of having time to rediscover each other is both invigorating and daunting. We have developed different interests with the passage of time. Our career choices are both servant-oriented, always giving out to others, often accompanied by high stress. With time, this has left its mark as we come home with nothing left to give, exhaustion prevailing. Our home has always been a place to just rest and be, and for that I am thankful.

The thing I have come to realize through all this is that the process of cleaning something up can sometimes be messy itself. Disorder, or disarray, is often part of the process of putting something together again. To go through the piles of stuff, both physically and metaphorically, all that kachi wachi has to be laid out so you can see everything. Only then can one go through piece by piece to figure out where it goes. More messes are made in the cleaning up process, but they are good and necessary.

The same goes for relationships. To go back and reexamine hurtful words spoken long ago. To see in a new light misplaced beliefs about the other person that began to take root at some point. To look at acquired habits that hindered the relationship rather than built it up. It all screams messy and needing attention. But there is life waiting to be discovered in this mess.

Something about the thought of cleaning up those messes and becoming clean gives me hope, anticipation for the future.

## Digging Deep

Are there relationships, even your marriage, where life has taken its toll? Has there been damage or neglect that has occurred due to the challenges of life? Maybe a lack of time or energy to work through conflict?

Putting the house together is becoming a priority. Not just for comfort's sake, but as a metaphor for those broken relationships we may experience. I am going into this new stage of life with just us two again and seeing it as a hunt for hidden treasure. Room by room, floor by floor. Rediscovering hidden gems in each other.

This may involve removing the carpet, prying up a plank, and, in the process, finding a long-lost love letter. I look forward to picking up the piles and finding that missing piece from a game we used to play or a picture from some cherished memory.

Most of our furniture is second-hand furniture handed down from family, which has been a blessing. But maybe, just maybe, it's time for our own new furniture. Instead of living off someone else's style, we can discover our own. Anticipation of exploring new interests and hobbies together stirs excitement within.

It will be messy and involve work, but hope springs up when I think of all the treasure just waiting to be found.

# 5

# THE TATTOO

I find myself voluntarily lying on a table waiting for a needle to penetrate my skin, injecting ink inside.

The piercing commences and continues for the next hour and a half. I practice deep breathing like I am in labor to make it through the pain and not move. I do not have a high pain tolerance. As the needle finds its way closer and closer to my ankle, the pain is almost unbearable. I find out later this is one of the most painful parts of the body in which to place a tattoo.

Why did I put myself through this? Humans can be strange creatures, and I am no exception.

When I turned fifty, I gifted myself with a tattoo on the bottom of my right leg. It is a watercolor painting of two flowers whose stems are wrapped around each other. The word going up the side of the stems is "entwined." The Hebrew translation of the word entwined found in Isaiah 26:8 carries the meaning of waiting.

Waiting on God until my heart is one with his, so entwined that one cannot tell where one begins and the other ends.

It was a big deal for me to make this decision and act on it. I had always admired images on other people's skin and thought it would be fun to have my own. Something harmless like a dolphin or turtle swimming around my ankle, just a small drawing. But I could feel the disapproval from those around me, the perceived negative stigma of having a tattoo.

Ironically, that is also what drove me to get one. I was tired of having to "fit inside the box" of a "good girl." I wanted to break outside this mold of how others viewed me.

But a deeper reason grew from a word given to me by a friend. I was told I reminded them of Peter the apostle. Peter in the sense that he was the first to jump in the lake to walk toward Jesus. He was one of the first disciples to take risks in his passion to follow Jesus and share who Jesus was with others.

I have lived most of my life being quiet about my faith. So, when I was given this word that I was like Peter, my first reaction was of deep sadness. My being quiet was similar to Peter's denying Jesus and keeping my faith to myself for fear of what others might think of me.

I wanted to be true to myself and grow in boldness. Hence, the idea of etching a permanent design on my body started to take a deeper meaning. A simple sea creature was no longer enough. When I saw my friend's drawings of flowers with the word "entwined," I knew. It still took me a year to get the courage and take the plunge.

The experience was rather comical, looking back. God was more than aware that I have a low pain tolerance. In the tattoo parlor God provided me with the stories told by three men concerning a frequent visitor who was a very colorful character. Colorful to the point of taking my mind away from the pain of what was being done to my body because of the craziness of this man's life story.

## The Meaning of a Tattoo

This is the thing I have learned about tattoos: they are an open invitation to learning people's stories. It amazes me how people are more than willing to share the stories behind their tattoos when asked. What is sad is how many people don't ask simply because they do not approve. For some, the negative stigma is stronger than the desire to break down barriers and communicate.

It is interesting to me the responses I have received since getting a tattoo. I can tell those who disapprove when they immediately frown and change the conversation the moment they realize what I did. They don't ask why I did it. Then there are those who are genuinely curious and interested.

When I am asked, it is an open door to the gospel. I am able to share how the word "entwine" means to wait on God until his will becomes my will. This opens the door to share my story and how God has changed my life. I am being given a chance to rewrite all those past episodes where I chose to be quiet about my faith and am now learning to become bold.

My tattoo has also served as a source of encouragement in dark times. During my experience of walking some two hundred miles in Portugal and Spain, while dealing with the pain and exhaustion, at night I would wrap my hands around my tattooed leg and remind myself that God was with me. This reality was literally ingrained in my flesh. During the day when working through the pain of blisters and muscle spasms, a glance down at my flowers reminded me I was one with God in that moment. God was with me in my pain.

As I am now going through this school year, all I have to do is look down at my right leg to bring back to the forefront of my mind that God is with me. He is with me through the valleys, the storms, the raging seas. I will not drown.

**Digging Deep**

As I was pondering my tattoo, the thought of Jesus and the scars on his hands and feet came to mind. After his crucifixion they became part of his flesh. They are now a physical testament to his identity, his sacrifice and immense love for humanity. These scars show his heart and desire to be in relationship with us. They are permanently implanted in his flesh.

Likewise, my "entwined" flowers are now permanently a part of me, a part of my body, my testimony. The tattoo has become its own treasure in the unexpected encouragement it has brought me through this last year, including boldness and confidence I previously lacked.

I know I can't compare, but as Jesus was pierced for our sins, in a way I went through my own piercing pain, voluntarily, as a way to show Jesus my love and loyalty. It has brought me close to him. There is no other treasure greater than this.

I am not necessarily encouraging others to go get tattoos, but is there something you can do that is significant to you? Something to remind you of God's hand in your own life? Something that will remain?

The greatest thing you can do is decide to believe in God and follow him. Once this decision is made, you are permanently part of his family with an eternal home in heaven.

*"Yes, we will follow your ways, Lord YAHWEH,*
*And entwine our hearts with yours,*
*For the fame of your name is all we desire."*
Isaiah 26:8 (TPT)

# 6

# A BOILED EGG

One Sunday morning I was given a most extraordinary gift: a boiled egg. It wasn't an actual boiled egg, but the vision of God handing me a boiled egg.

My pastor, who gave it to me, was both baffled and amused. My first thought was that it seemed a bit funny and even plain, but obviously there was something there. I went home and began the process of unpacking the significance of a boiled egg and realized what a gift I had been given.

A boiled egg, as compared to a fried egg, contains fewer calories due to not using butter or oil to prepare it. A boiled egg is simply that, nothing else, unless one adds salt and pepper. It is one of the easiest and most nutritious additions to one's diet.

I looked up the attributes of a boiled egg and found numerous sites bursting with information. For example, an average egg contains only seventy-seven calories with six grams of high-quality protein and five grams of healthy fat. An egg is a powerhouse of iron, vitamins, minerals, and carotenoids. Carotenoids reduce the risk of disease, especially certain cancers and eye disease. The vitamins and minerals contained in an egg include vitamin D, all of the variants of vitamin B, zinc, and calcium—mostly in the yolk.

I proceeded to investigate further into each of these benefits. I found that the protein in eggs is easily digestible and absorbed by the body. This protein contains all the amino acids required by the body in the right proportions. Amino acids are essential for the growth and repair of tissues and muscles. They help in the production of hormones, support the immune system, and provide energy. That is just the protein!

Continuing on my quest for more information on the benefits of a boiled egg, I found eggs are good for weight loss since they fill one up and reduce hunger cravings. Brain health is boosted by lowering the risk of cognitive impairments and the effects of aging. Blood pressure and cholesterol are lowered. Eye health is boosted as the egg protects one against increased risk of macular degeneration and cataracts. Skin and hair improve from the consumption of eggs. Fetal development, especially in the area of brain and spinal cord cells, benefits from eggs. Mental health is affected because eggs help prevent depression.

Blown away by the overwhelming benefits of an egg, it was brought to my mind how they are also a universal food. Not one country has a monopoly on egg production. Chickens are raised everywhere, and the egg is a food most people eat. And even though vegans don't eat eggs, the egg crossed the restrictions of fitting within a vegetarian and most other diets.

It seemed to me the egg is a complete nutritional package. If one has access to eggs, one does not need to eat anything else. So I did some further investigation to see if they are fine for complete nutrition. What I discovered is that eggs are not a complete nutritional package. Despite being loaded with health benefits, they lack important nutrients found in other foods. For example, there is no vitamin C found in eggs. Vitamin C plays a role in boosting the immune system to control and fight infections.

I confess I don't eat boiled eggs all that regularly. But one of the times I do eat a boiled egg is the morning of a race. It provides me with the protein needed and is easy to digest.

Putting this all together I started to ponder the significance of everything I had learned regarding a boiled egg, especially thinking of it as a food I eat before a race. There are many passages in the Bible that allude to life being a race or, more specifically, to how we each have our own race to run.

## Community Is Our Vitamin C

Hebrews 12:1 (niv): "Let us throw off everything that hinders and the sin that so easily entangles. And let us run with perseverance the race that is marked out for us."

In order to run our race, we need to persevere. That is where eggs come in. Spiritual eggs. These eggs include spending time with God, reading the Bible, praying, and just being in his presence. These actions that the eggs represent enable one to throw off those things that hinder our walk and slow us down.

They empower us to be free from the sin that keeps coming back to tempt us.

But that is not enough.

Eggs are not complete nutrition. We need others! God created us for community. We can't run our race on our own but need others to come alongside us. The people who run with us are like our Vitamin C. We build one another up through encouragement. Our spiritual immune system is stronger with others coming alongside helping us fight off what comes against us to destroy us—the infections. We help each other fight against the enemy, whether that be depression, loneliness, doubt, persecution, etc.

The Prayer of St. Francis has always struck a deep chord within me. It tells us that where there is hatred, offense, doubt, despair, sadness, we are to bring love, forgiveness, faith, hope, joy. It is all about community and allowing God to work through us to show his love to others as well as to allow others to bless us. It is all about being an instrument of God's peace. It is about shining a light in the darkness of people's lives and bringing them hope.

It is a prayer of dying to oneself in order to lift others up. Instead of seeking to be consoled, consoling others. Instead of seeking to be understood, striving to understand. It is about loving others, even if this love is not reciprocated.

We find that as we live this way, we receive as we give out. We find ourselves in the midst of self-forgetting. We are forgiven in the act of forgiving others.

Back to where I am currently in this time of life. This Prayer of St. Francis has had a huge impact on me. It helps guide me in how I want to live my life, intentionally reaching out to others. But what happens when I have nothing to give? When there is literally nothing to pour out? What if I find myself depleted of Vitamin C to pass on to others?

The gift of a boiled egg is incredibly valuable. But we need more. We need each other. At this particular time in my life, I don't feel I have much to give out to those around me. When I find myself with some time, I simply don't find the energy to reach out and share, even with those closest to me. I wouldn't even know how to start.

It has occurred to me that writing this book is for this reason. It is a way to share, even though I am not receiving at the moment. But, then again, I am receiving something as I write. Confirmation of my feelings? Maybe it's about me giving back to myself right now. Giving myself this time to reflect and write, because I, too, am valuable. Maybe this is God's way of giving me my boiled egg and, for this period, providing for all my needs, including my Vitamin C, knowing it will be given out to others in due time.

## Digging Deep

Recently I heard a man speak about our seasons of life. We are often surprised to find ourselves in a season of winter and wonder how we got there. We are still in our summer clothes and not prepared. However, winter is needed. Winter is not a time to plant seeds, but a time to rest. Sleep. Recuperate. Focus on spending time with God. Focus on being with family.

I am slowly coming to realize that God is telling me I am in a winter season. And it's okay. I am beginning to embrace putting on my cozy warm sweatpants and fluffy socks. The water has been put on to boil for a hot drink, and the fireplace turned on. Bible and journal lie waiting on the table.

Maybe, just maybe, this book is my "pleasant pool," my own "brook of blessing" that, in time, I can pour out to others (Psalm 84:5–7, TPT). For now, I will be content with my boiled egg. God is telling me that he is enough for me.

Who knew a boiled egg could be such a treasure?

# 7

# THE GRIP

A young woman often attended our Friday night gatherings. When the evening gatherings turned into Sunday morning church, her family was there every week, very involved in the beginning of the new church. She kept to herself, seated with her family, not often talking with others. Her name was Kasey.

I had been struggling inside with a burden I have been carrying for a long time. It would come and go, some days stronger than others. On this particular Sunday, the burden felt heavy. At the end of the service when those of us needing prayer were invited to stand, I stood, communicating I needed prayer.

Kasey was sitting in front of me. She turned around and grabbed my wrist. She had one of the strongest grips I had ever experienced, and she held on as the church started interceding. This firm grip was one of the most comforting sensations I have ever felt. It touched my soul in a deep place that has stayed with me since.

God communicated to me through this grip that He was not letting go of my life. He had me firmly in His grasp. When I read or recall verses about His grip, Kasey's holding onto me comes to mind.

Isaiah 41:13 (TPT): "I grip your right hand *and won't let you go!*"

Hebrews 13:5 (TPT): "I will never leave you, never! And I will not loosen my grip on your life!"

Along with these verses, I read Psalm 46:10 (NLT): "Be still, and know that I am God!" I am to rest in this.

Romans 5:17 (TPT) says we are held in the grip of his grace. Something about this compels me to dig deeper.

Then I find it. I strike gold!

Grace. It covers us. Second Corinthians 12:9 tells us that God's grace is more than enough for us and covers our weaknesses. All our mistakes, even those we haven't made yet, are already covered by his grace! Grace that can turn everything into good in our lives, even things that have harmed us. Grace provides us with the strength to overcome every situation life presents us. Grace is defined as undeserved favor. It is something that cannot be earned but shows God's heart towards us. If we allow it to, grace guides us to the heart of God and who God says we are.

"Yes, God is more than ready to overwhelm you with every form of grace, so that you will have more than enough of everything —every moment and in every way. He will make you overflow with abundance in every good thing you do" (2 Corinthians 9:8, TPT).

## Grace That Doesn't Let Go

I start to allow the truth of this to soak through my tired and worn-down soul. I am held in this grip of grace that promises me he is more than enough for me.

For my fiftieth birthday, a friend gifted me with a box containing fifty words. Grace pours out from these words as they remind me who I am in Christ, my true identity. I find, as I meditate on these words, they are part of recognizing this grip God has on my life, on me.

An image of the boiled egg pops into my brain.

Now that I am in this place of feeling frozen, I am holding onto this promise from God more than ever. In my evenings when I return home full of discouragement and low energy and can't seem to do anything, it's okay. I don't know exactly what I am facing, but I am to rest. I am to have hope and live in the expectation that God knows exactly what I am dealing with and will provide more than enough for my needs.

Grace controls and directs all negatives to a place where they are utterly defeated. These words in my box are powerful and challenge all the negatives I have believed about myself. They help counteract all the negative perspectives and mindsets I have entertained. This grace tells me I am more than enough because he is with me. I am to walk into every situation knowing what I have is already sufficient. All because of the fullness of his heart toward me.

Five words for today.

Kristin, you are: Renewed. Pure. Complete. Hopeful. Creative.

Take hold of who God says you are, and don't let go. It may not feel like it, but this is reality. Learn to view what you are facing through this reality.

In the meantime, I am to rest in his grip. This amazing, unbelievable grip of grace.

## Digging Deep

Are there situations in your life where you are overcome by discouragement? Areas where hope is missing? Things you believe about yourself that are not from God?

I challenge you to picture yourself being gripped by God. Gripped by his grace. This may look different to each of us. The image could be one of being held in his hand, or him holding onto your hand. Regardless, see yourself as being held onto tightly. As you are held in this grip, allow his love to pour in and remind you of who you truly are.

I was recently pressed to write down all those negatives I believed about myself on one side of a piece of paper. On the other side, I wrote what God said about me using words from my word box. As I went through this exercise, I could feel my mindset being renewed. Negatives being washed away, turning into positives. Grace in action. This exercise has been extremely helpful for me in this process of renewing my mind. I encourage you to try it.

What words is God speaking to you right now? What words is he using to tell you who you are?

Can you picture yourself being held in his grip?

# 8

# THE BRICK WALL

More feelings of hopelessness wash over me as I receive yet another email presenting more barriers to this mother trying to get help for her son.

It started last spring when I was contacted by the director of a Special Education Department of one of our local school districts. A family was in need of help in knowing where to turn and learn more about a possible CVI (cortical visual impairment) diagnosis for their son. He was already receiving services for autism and ADHD, but the interventions were not working for him. Something was missing, and this mom was desperate for help.

After talking with her on the phone, I sent her a CVI screener to see if, indeed, CVI could describe her son's behavior. After filling out the screening, her response was amazement that it was the first questionnaire that really described her child. Hope was rekindled that her son could finally get the support he needed.

I proceeded to write a letter to accompany the CVI screener she would then take to the eye doctor as our service require a report and diagnosis from an eye doctor. Unfortunately, the one doctor she went to had a huge misunderstanding regarding CVI and refused to give a diagnosis.

A brick wall.

As I explain in my book *Gifts of Sight* and on my website Vistaquest.org, cortical/cerebral visual impairment is the leading cause of visual impairment in the world, and the most misunderstood. This family had the misfortune of being assigned to a doctor who had not kept up with the latest research on CVI. Unfortunately, Oregon law also posed a barrier in that a diagnosis is required for services to be given.

At first glance, this makes sense.

But when it comes to CVI, other states are ahead of the game and understand how students can fall through the cracks with this particular law in place. In most states, if there is impact shown due to visual impairment, services are to be provided regardless of the presence of a diagnosis.

This can also be abused, but it acts as a safeguard to ensure students, like this boy, receive the support they need to be able to access learning at the same level as their typically sighted peers.

The current law in Oregon was another brick wall.

## Breaking the Wall

The presence of these brick walls makes me doubt myself and my ability to make a difference in the lives of my students. Do I try to fight the brick wall? What can I do when up against the written word of a medical doctor? When up against the written letter of the law? Hope feels like it is slipping away. I can't even imagine what this parent is feeling at this moment.

How does one cope when all the odds seem to be against them?

God shows himself, again. Through Kasey, who gripped my arm so tightly that Sunday morning in church. This is what happened after she let go.

Kasey, who had been gripping my arm, turned to me after the prayer and started talking to me. She told me she saw me facing a brick wall. The wall was something I could not break or penetrate and was something I had been facing a long time. In the vision Kasey saw this huge monster truck come up from behind me smashing the wall to smithereens. I was not to fear. Rather, I was to rest in faith and trust that God was taking care of that brick wall.

## Hope Rekindled

Today I was able to experience God's faithfulness in his words to me.

The blankness in my brain gave way to a shaft of light. Some creativity came to me throughout the course of the day, taking me a few steps forward in my planning for a student. A dim light shining where there was only darkness in my mind. I grabbed hold of that light and, as I followed it, the light slowly grew brighter.

I have a preschooler who is ready to learn pre-braille skills. The challenge is she attends a Montesorri preschool where direct instruction is not the method used; rather, exploration is encouraged. "Works" are provided for the students to learn on their own. However, when it comes to working with students who have a significant visual impairment, they don't have the benefit of incidental learning. Incidental learning is the learning that just happens naturally from observing the world around us. My students need direct instruction since they don't have the same amount of access to this type of learning as typically sighted children.

The challenge I was faced with was how to provide the teaching in the skills my student needs in this particular preschool environment. How do I support this type of exploratory learning and ensure my student is getting what is necessary for acquiring pre-braille skills?

Completion of the project: laminated ABC cards with braille cells presenting the letters both in print and in braille. My student has sufficient vision to be able to see the large red letters in print and the colored two-inch circles of the braille cell. A muffin tin with six cups accompanies the letter card. Perfect for representing the braille cell. Tennis balls with VELCRO® to attach to the bottom of the muffin cups are included. Put it all together and my student has a "work," using the Montessori vocabulary. The goal is to grab a laminated card and then replicate the letter in the muffin tin using the tennis balls. All part of building that conceptual framework needed to learn braille.

God has shown His faithfulness again. This particular brick wall is down. A small glimmer of hope begins to burn. I will grab hold of it and bring it before the other brick walls facing me.

## Digging Deep

We all have walls in our lives. Walls that act as barriers to something we may want to accomplish, or a relationship we may be experiencing. What walls are you facing at this time of your life? Are you waiting for a monster truck to come take it down?

I encourage you, that monster truck will come, just as it has countless times throughout the ages. Just as it did for Moses, Elijah, David, Esther, Ruth, Peter, Paul, etc. The list goes on and on.

As I wait for my own personal brick wall to come down, a friend points out to me that maybe, for right now, this wall is up for my protection. I am learning that there may be different purposes concerning each wall or barrier.

I think back to my Camino trip and the picture on the cover of this book. I am walking flanked on either side by walls. These walls keep me from going in the wrong direction. Perhaps from going off a cliff. They protect me.

And yet another friend brought to my attention the story of Joseph, who was referred to as a fruitful vine, growing by a spring, that climbed over the wall. Despite flaming arrows being shot at him, Joseph was able to keep climbing that wall because he was well fed from the spring and he knew he would reach the other side (See Genesis 49:22).

And then I read, "Can't you see? I have carved your name on the palms of my hands! Your walls are always my concern" (Isaiah 49:16, TPT).

In Isaiah 54:12, God talks about all our walls being made of precious stones. Our struggles are precious to God because they can bring us closer to him.

Something more to think about. Isn't that like God? To be so protective and loving toward us? Is it possible you are looking at your brick wall through the wrong lens? Sometimes it takes another perspective to come to that awareness and view that brick wall from a different angle. More treasure found.

# GIFT OF HOPE

Last week I received an email that broke my heart. Caroline had passed away. This little girl had cortical visual impairment and benefitted from using my BaseKit. I never met Caroline, who was only two and a half when she died. Somehow, by the grace of God, I had the honor of playing a part in her short life.

The previous year I had created a raffle to give away one of my VistaQuest BaseKits to a loving family. I had numerous responses from all over the country. As did several others, this one family's response particularly touched me to the core, and they were chosen as the recipient of this prize.

A little about Caroline.

Caroline spent her first year of life in the hospital on dialysis after having both kidneys removed because she was born with a rare kidney disease. During this time, due to an infection and unchecked blood pressure, Caroline had a stroke that left her with cortical visual impairment. A trach and vent aiding her in breathing and eating, along with the peritoneal dialysis, were a daily reality.

As Caroline moved back home, her family and team of therapists worked together to make life easier for her, but there were still barriers they did not know how to cross. Barriers of how to actively engage her, involving questions of how much she could see and understand what she was seeing.

Caroline's response to the BaseKit overwhelmed me when I first read what her mom wrote. Her therapists had started incorporating the tools and activities into what they did with her. Caroline's siblings, nine and five years old, were able to pick a Trail Guide card from the kit with the item it went with and play with Caroline. Interactions were occurring more and more.

Caroline's absolute favorite item was the golden pinwheel. When it was set up beside her, her face would light up and her mouth would open wide, her whole body wiggling as if she wanted to get it. Through use of the BaseKit, Caroline learned how to use her limited vision to better understand her world.

Motivation increased, and Caroline was tolerating her stretches and exercises so much better with the right setup and environment. Her physical therapist, occupational therapist, and speech therapist were all using the BaseKit, incorporating it into their therapy.

Over the last year, I would get other updates on Caroline and how well she was still responding to the BaseKit. When I felt discouraged about how my own slow progress with students, I would read back through these emails and think about Caroline.

This was my "why" for what I do. My purpose.

When I received the news of her death, my heart fell. I had this hope that one day I would meet Caroline and her lovely family. How can the passing of someone I had never met have such a big impact on me?

I turn back to the motto of my VistaQuest business: "Hope is not the conviction that something will turn out well, but the certainty that something is worth doing no matter how it turns out." (Attributed to Václav Havel in various writings and speeches).

Caroline's mom, Hallie, wrote to me after her little girl died, thanking me for "the big part I played in giving her a beautiful life." Me. Through my actions, I opened up a new world for this precious little girl and touched not only her life, but those of her family and therapists as they watched Caroline engage with her world with joy.

Only this was not me, but God working through me. God who gifted me with the mind to think the way I do. The heart to reach out and help others. I couldn't do this on my own. Any of it.

It came to me while processing the news of Caroline's death. I didn't want to say goodbye. I wanted her to live on. She had no idea how her life impacted mine, and I couldn't let that go.

With the help of my business coach, we came up with a way to continue to honor Caroline's life and spread her light to others.

This will be done through gifting a family with either a BaseKit of their own or personal training in setting up CVI strategies in the home. Through these methods, Caroline will continue to bless others and spread hope.

## Digging Deep

Are there areas in your life where you need hope? Hope that things will get better. A situation where you have waited for something good to happen for a long time? A relationship that is waiting for reconciliation? I encourage you to not give up and to keep moving forward, no matter how bleak the present may seem.

Throughout this journey we call life, I have learned that hope is birthed through suffering. Romans sums it up well: "We also glory in our sufferings, because we know that suffering produces perseverance, perseverance, character; and character, hope" (Romans 5:3–4, NIV).

Through it all, we don't know how it will turn out. I don't know how the rest of this present school year will turn out. I don't know if that one family encountering numerous brick walls will ever get the help they need for their son. I don't know if the burden I carry will be lightened. My house still has piles of flooring with little progress. I don't know when it will be completed.

But we continue forward because of hope. Hope that what we are doing is worthwhile, no matter the results.

This sums it up for me. And maybe this is what it is all truly about. Life. Following God. Seeking the treasure of his life in oneself. Treasure that turns into hope, which in turn becomes faith that has been shaped and molded through tribulations and perseverance through all those dark times in life.

# EPILOGUE

As I have been writing this book, and editing, and writing more, and editing more, the image of a diamond comes to mind. Diamonds are formed deep beneath the ground, between ninety to 150 miles down in the earth's mantle. They are the result of carbon atoms being squeezed together under extreme pressure and heat. Some diamonds can be found closer to the surface due to erosion, but typically one has to dig deep to find the diamonds that are formed underground.

The diamonds found at the deepest depths are among those considered most valuable. The deeper the depth, the more intense the pressure and heat are. This intensity causes higher quality in clarity, color, and size. That being said, the value placed on a diamond is also determined by the cut, carat, clarity, and color, which is not necessarily determined by how far underground they are found.

The metaphor of digging deep for diamonds resonates with me. It goes back to that introspection, the inner soul-searching that is needed to get through tough times. It's that summoning every bit of strength and effort we have within us to overcome something.

When we go through trials, we are also under pressure. This pressure can take on many forms. It can be the result of bad decisions or something outside our control, such as an ice storm or the death of a loved one. Maybe you feel squeezed into a corner, trapped in a relationship where you feel powerless to bring about change.

The thing is, this pressure brings about resilience and character. "A diamond in the rough" means a diamond that has potential, but at the moment is still rough and lacking refinement. Through the forging process, the diamond gains value and becomes beautiful. Clarity and color are manifested, beauty brought to light.

Going back to Romans 5:3–4, The Passion Translation uses the word "pressures" for the challenges we go through: "Even in times of trouble we have a joyful confidence, knowing that our pressures will develop in us patient endurance. And patient endurance will refine our character, and proven character leads us back to hope."

**Pressure**

As we go through our times of trouble, we learn how to endure and be patient, which, in turn, refines our character and brings about hope. These trials we endure have the potential to create a beautiful stone.

Maybe, just maybe, you will discover among all the riches found in your particular journey that you are part of the treasure, a brilliant diamond.

I don't know where you find yourself in this time of your life, what season you are in. I started writing this book knowing that when I finished, I might still be in the thick of it. I might still be experiencing the struggle of winter. I am learning to be okay with this. We are not meant to walk this journey alone. I have found treasures in my journey—the ability to endure hard things, the experience of being entwined with God through it all, the grip of grace, an infinite invitation to rest, the gift of community. One of the biggest gems I have discovered through all my personal sufferings can be summed up in one word. Hope.

For some reason, I was meant to share my own struggles along this journey we call life. Maybe it is to show you that you are not alone. We all go through periods of life where we face our own brick walls. Maybe, like me, you don't know exactly what they are, just that those walls are there.

In the meantime, keep walking. Step by step, even if it is baby steps. Don't forget to look up and appreciate the beauty around you. It is there, even if you have to search a little. You may not be able to see very far ahead of you, but it's going to be okay. There may be walls around you. You are to rest knowing God sees the whole picture and is already well-acquainted with what you are facing. For right now, know you have it in you to dig deep. As you dig, treasure will be found. It is there now, waiting for you to discover.

Will you join in the search?

# ABOUT THE AUTHOR

As a child, Kristin Gault knew that when she grew up, she wanted to help people. Raised in Bolivia, the daughter of missionary parents, she experienced first-hand the needs of people often forgotten in their own context. Her relationship to Jesus, beginning in childhood and growing through adulthood, strengthened the commitment of reaching out to others.

Back home in the US, Kristin completed her bachelor's degree in sociology/social work, thinking this might open doors to work with people. But as she and her husband, Jon, lived overseas the first four years of their marriage, she discovered how much she loved teaching. She went back to school to get a degree in elementary education and then taught a blended 4th/5th grade classroom for five years. During this time, her own children were born. The diagnosis of her two sons, Reilly and Peter, with visual impairments propelled her back to school for a second master's degree that would enable her to become a Teacher for the Visually Impaired (TVI).

Kristin has been a TVI in Oregon since 2012. She has specialized training in cortical/cerebral visual impairment (CVI) and provides assessments, interventions, and strategies for students with this condition throughout Lane County. Beyond her TVI role, Kristin is co-chair of the statewide Oregon

CVI Team and has run trainings throughout the Pacific Northwest both with a team and on her own. Kristin's hands-on experience and research inspired her to create VistaQuest and its intervention tool, the BaseKit, geared especially for students with CVI. This tool is now being used throughout the United States and is spreading to other countries.

Kristin and her husband are parents to three amazing children, two who are now adults and one in high school. Being a parent to two sons with disabilities has given Kristin the ability to connect with the families she works with. She understands their unique challenges and the need to advocate for one's child. She understands the importance of making sure her daughter, who does not have a disability, is also seen and heard.

Kristin has a bachelor's in sociology/social work from George Fox University, a master's in elementary education from Pacific University, and a master's in becoming a Teacher for the Visually Impaired from University of Northern Colorado), and specialized training in CVI from Perkins University.

Kristin's websites:

VistaQuest.org

KristinGault.com

# ACKNOWLEDGEMENTS

Starting in order from the beginning of 2024:

First and foremost, I want to thank my husband, Jon. Your tireless work and determination to keep us, our pets, and our property safe during the ice storm and the following months show your servant's heart. As life changes for us and our kids are growing up and moving out, I look forward to going on treasure hunts together discovering more about each other.

To the Thomas family: Austin, Tiffany, Cameron, Hailey, and Evan. You are some of the most generous people I know. The type of friends one can call for help, who will stop whatever you are doing and come. Thank you for stepping out, again, and giving us a place to stay those first few days during and after the ice storm, and for all your support and expertise in helping put our home back together.

To Matt and Beth Matthews: Thank you for opening up your garage for our dogs when you heard about our need and your willingness to keep them a few days, even after Rumble ran away. You guys are the best!

To John and Stephanie Lovdokken: You opened up your home to Peter and me for the six months following the storm. You provided us a place to stay where we felt completely welcomed and safe. You guys have become like family, and we love you!

To all the family and friends who prayed for us and reached out during this time. We felt surrounded by love.

To my EC Cares family who surprised me with their thoughtfulness and support after the ice storm.

To Heather, my Camino soulmate: We both know I couldn't have made it to Santiago without your help and support. I love you!

To Soorin: for being faithful in giving me the gift of a boiled egg. We were both amused at the time, but I had no idea how much I would need that boiled egg!

To Kasey: Thank you for being faithful in turning around and gripping my hand and then sharing what the Holy Spirit wanted to tell me. It has made a huge impact on my life and brought me much hope!

To Hallie: Words cannot express how much it means that I was able to play a part in Caroline's life. She was so blessed with a family who would do anything for her, and I could tell she was a joy to all she came in contact with. Thank you.

To Jesse and Elisheba: Your support and belief in my writing means the world! Elisheba, thank you for being receptive to the Holy Spirit knowing I had another book I needed to write before delving deep into one I had planned on El Camino.